this book belongs to us:

XOX

(doodle a portrait of yourselves,
or jot down your names)

ME, YOU, US

a book to fill out together

Lisa Currie

A Perigee Book

A PERIGEE BOOK
Published by the Penguin Group
Penguin Group (USA) LLC
375 Hudson Street, New York, New York 10014

USA • Canada • UK • Ireland • Australia • New Zealand • India • South Africa • China

penguin.com

A Penguin Random House Company

ME, YOU, US

ISBN: 978-0-399-16794-2

First edition: June 2014

PRINTED IN THE UNITED STATES OF AMERICA

20 19 18 17 16

dedicated to my sweet, hilarious
friends who I hope to doodle
on these pages with soon.

xox

welcome to ME, YOU, US—
the book to fill out together.

Yep. Together! This is a creative space to share with your friends or a loved one.

- Write fortune cookie messages to each other!
- Decide on your perfect theme song!
- Doodle a portrait together!
- Brainstorm ideas for your matching tattoos!

Fill out each page with a different friend, or complete the whole book with a special someone. Invite your pals, your partner, your brother, your whole family, or all of your classmates to join. And the best part? As you create it, ME, YOU, US will become an amazing time capsule to look back on and treasure. *

So who will you share this book with?
Find your plus-one (or two) and enjoy your "us time" together!

xox lisa

P.S. more hints to get started on the next page...

* Idea: Once you've filled out every page together, wrap your book with paper and string (like a birthday present) and stick on a label that says "NO PEEKING FOR ONE YEAR". Then pop it in the back of your closet or under your bed. Done! Now twelve months later (or whenever you need a splash of happy thoughts) just unwrap the time capsule and enjoy your sweet nostalgia!

supply list

Pens are a good place to start. But why not get extra playful? Rustle up some colored pencils and markers. Find that set of glitter pens you once bought. Share your favorite art supplies with each other. Even collect magazines and photos to cut out and scrapbook over the pages.

Also a pot of tea and two mugs would be nice!

how to begin

In this book there are no rules and definetly no such thing as a wrong answer. Just flip to a random page and use the prompts to jot down whatever silly thoughts or sweet memories pop into your brain. Chat about it together. Or just doodle quietly, side by side. Non-awkward silences can be the best, no?

At the top of each page, there's a space (ME: You: us:) to write your names. Use the "us" part to explain how you know each other or create a nickname for yourselves, such as "the two amigos," "dance floor ninjas," or "the cheesecake crew." Yep. You get the idea.

table for two?

Each page in this book is designed for a twosome to complete together. That's you + someone else: four hands, two brains, one book. Maybe you've never collaborated with a friend, or maybe you have. Just relax and have fun with it. Chat together. Listen to each other. And don't be shy to finish each other's scribble or sentence .... that's the fun part!

BONUS TIP: If you want to get extra-crafty, glue an unsealed envelope to the inside cover of your book. It's the perfect place to collect little mementos together, like love notes and photobooth photos.

a few suggestions

- **For Best Friends:** keep this book in your bag and fill out a page every time you see each other. Imagine how quickly you'll fill it up.

- **For Families:** take this book along to your next family gathering. Ask everyone to pair up and fill out a page together. It'll make for a unique (and maybe hilarious!) family keepsake.

- **For Newlyweds:** keep this book on your nightstand and use it as a cute bedtime ritual to record your first year together.

- **For Travelers:** tuck this book into your backpack! Keep it as a journal to remember new friends or pass the time on your next road trip.

- **For Classmates:** ask all of your friends to fill out a page together. Then everyone can write little notes on the book cover!

ALL MY FAVORITE PEOPLE

You can share this book with just one special person, of course. But if you'd like to create a memento with a whole BUNCH of your favorite people, make a list of their names and check them off as you go.

Who I want to spend "us time" with:

- ☐ _____
- ☐ _____
- ☐ _____
- ☐ _____
- ☐ _____
- ☐ _____
- ☐ _____
- ☐ _____

Grab your first teammate and let's begin!

the story of how we met

*O*nce upon a time...

ME: _____   WHEN: _____

You: _____   WHERE: _____

US: _____

ME: _____ WHEN: _____

You: _____ WHERE: _____

US: _____

if a genie gave us three wishes

FIRST WISH

SECOND WISH

THIRD WISH

ME: _____   WHEN: _____

YOU: _____   WHERE: _____

US: _____

the perfect team name for us

ME: _____ WHEN: _____

YOU: _____ WHERE: _____

US: _____

pie chart of how we spend our time together

ME: _____ WHEN: _____

YOU: _____ WHERE: _____

US: _____

the dinner party
of our dreams

guest list

- you
- me
-
-
-
-
-
-

ME: _____ WHEN: _____

YOU: _____ WHERE: _____

US: _____

nice things we can do for each other

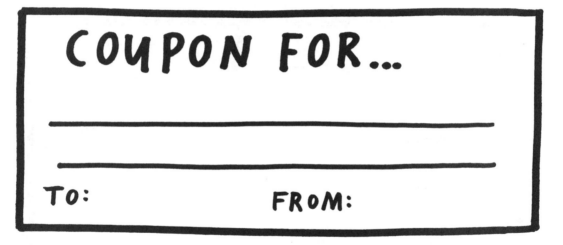

COUPON FOR...

_____

_____

TO: FROM:

COUPON FOR...

_____

_____

TO: FROM:

ME: _____   WHEN: _____

You: _____   WHERE: _____

US: _____

the last time we got REALLY EXCITED!!

ME: _____   WHEN: _____

YOU: _____   WHERE: _____

US: _____

we couldn't have done it without each other...

ME: _____ WHEN: _____

You: _____ WHERE: _____

US: _____

our recent chat on the phone

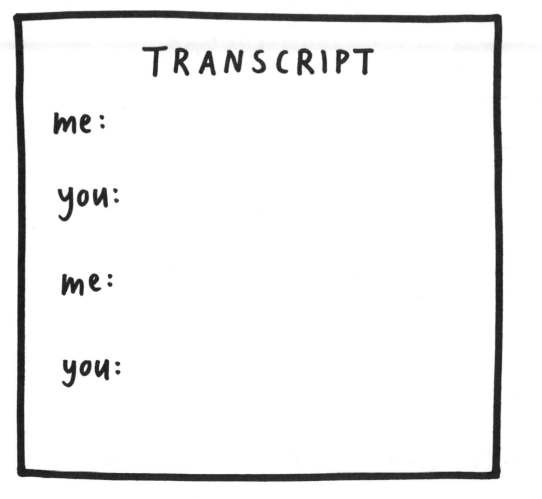

TRANSCRIPT

me:

you:

me:

you:

ME: _____ WHEN: _____

You: _____ WHERE: _____

US: _____

a poem about us

roses are red
violets are blue

ME: _____ WHEN: _____

YOU: _____ WHERE: _____

US: _____

the last time we made each other laugh

HAHAHA!! ☺ HA!

ME: _____ WHEN: _____

You: _____ WHERE: _____

US: _____

#hashtags about you and me

 _____

 _____

 _____

_____

* the longer the better!

ME: _____ WHEN: _____
You: _____ WHERE: _____
US: _____

reasons we'd stay up
all night together

1.

2.

3.

ME: _____   WHEN: _____

YOU: _____   WHERE: _____

US: _____

the cheapest fun
we've had together

TOTAL $

ME: _____ WHEN: _____

You: _____ WHERE: _____

US: _____

how we'd like to change the world

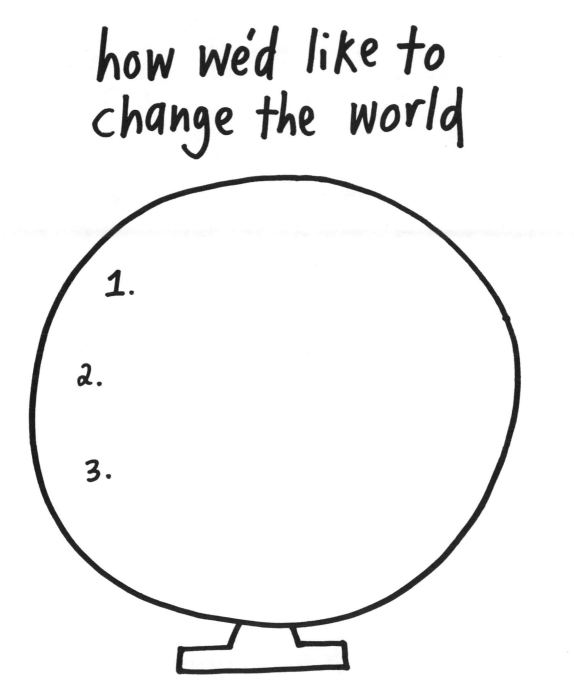

1.

2.

3.

ME: _____   WHEN: _____

YOU: _____   WHERE: _____

US: _____

how I'd describe you
to a stranger

ME: _____   WHEN: _____

You: _____   WHERE: _____

US: _____

the AMAZING act we could do in a talent show

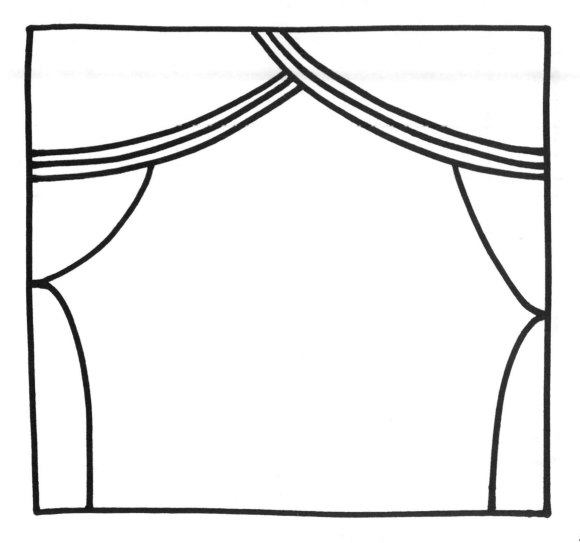

ME: _____   WHEN: _____

YOU: _____   WHERE: _____

US: _____

if we shared a bedroom

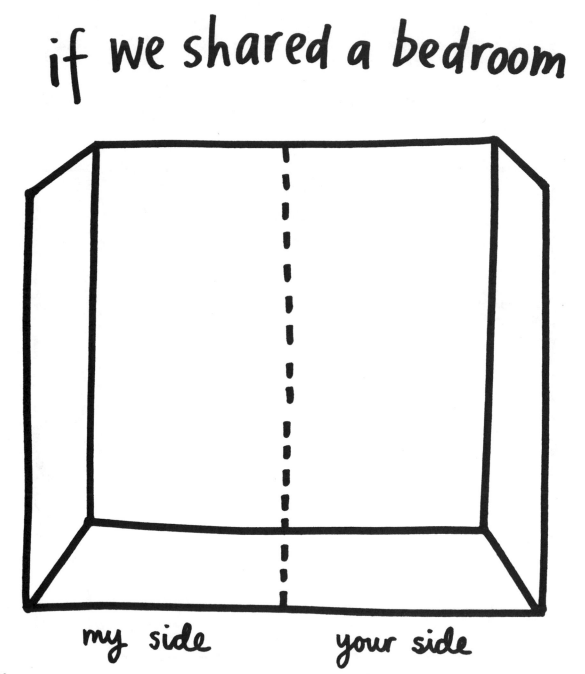

my side   your side

ME: _____   WHEN: _____
You: _____   WHERE: _____
US: _____

what people must think when they see us together

1.

2.

3.

how we pointed each other in the right direction

ME: _____ WHEN: _____

YOU: _____ WHERE: _____

US: _____

ME: _____   WHEN: _____

YOU: _____   WHERE: _____

US: _____

brands that best describe "us"

UNOFFICIAL
SPONSORS

-
-
-

ME: _____   WHEN: _____

You: _____   WHERE: _____

US: _____

our unusual talents

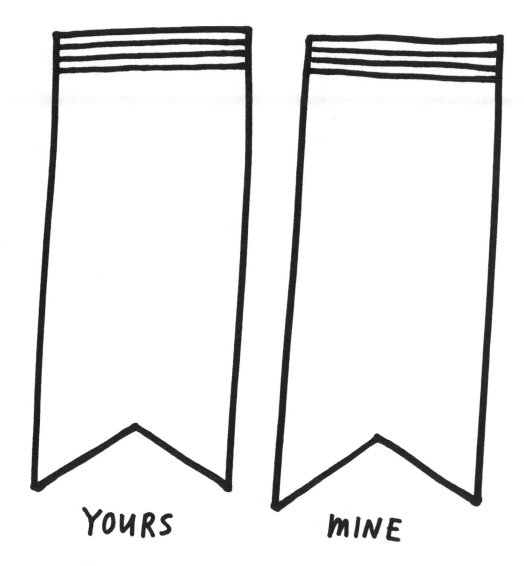

YOURS   MINE

ME: _____   WHEN: _____

You: _____   WHERE: _____

US: _____

your best party trick

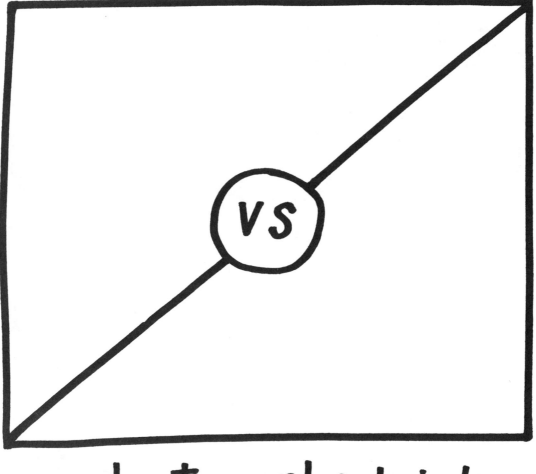

VS

my best party trick

ME: _____ WHEN: _____

YOU: _____ WHERE: _____

US: _____

tiny details we notice about each other

ME: _____ WHEN: _____

You: _____ WHERE: _____

US: _____

if we made our own
public holiday

DAY!

how to celebrate:

1.

2.

3.

ME: _____ WHEN: _____

You: _____ WHERE: _____

US: _____

an epic conversation we had*

* drawn from memory

ME: _____ WHEN: _____

You: _____ WHERE: _____

US: _____

things that happen in our fantasyland

1.

2.

3.

ME: _____ WHEN: _____

YOU: _____ WHERE: _____

US: _____

the book we could use right now

HOW TO

ME: _____ WHEN: _____

You: _____ WHERE: _____

US: _____

places we've had the most fun together

N

ME: _____   WHEN: _____

YOU: _____   WHERE: _____

US: _____

ways we refuse to grow up

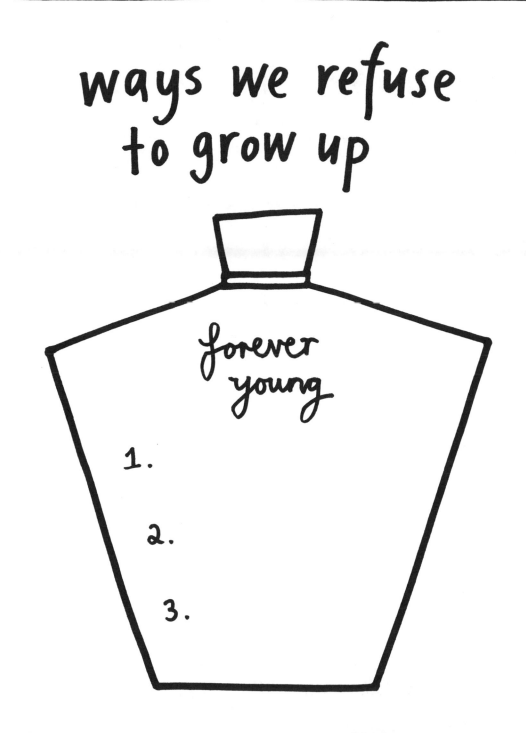

forever young

1.

2.

3.

ME: _____   WHEN: _____

YOU: _____   WHERE: _____

US: _____

things we recently learned about each other

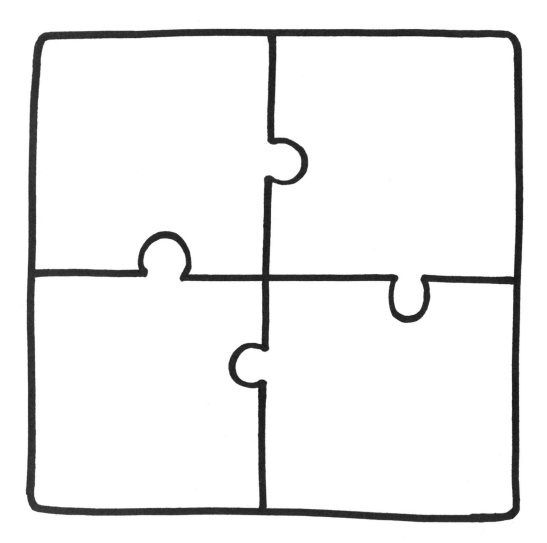

ME: _____   WHEN: _____
You: _____   WHERE: _____
US: _____

the perfect theme song for us

OPTION A

OPTION B

the things that remind me of you

I SPY...

ME: _____ WHEN: _____

You: _____ WHERE: _____

US: _____

I SPY...

ME: _____ WHEN: _____

YOU: _____ WHERE: _____

US: _____

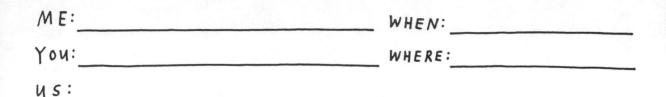

details of our day together

taste

smell

touch

sound

ME: _____ WHEN: _____

You: _____ WHERE: _____

US: _____

the characters we pretend to be

ME: _____   WHEN: _____

YOU: _____   WHERE: _____

US: _____

our secret ingredient

that makes everything better

ME: _____ WHEN: _____

You: _____ WHERE: _____

US: _____

the last time we were partners in crime

WANTED

FOR:

ME: _____ WHEN: _____

YOU: _____ WHERE: _____

US: _____

the best advice we ever gave each other

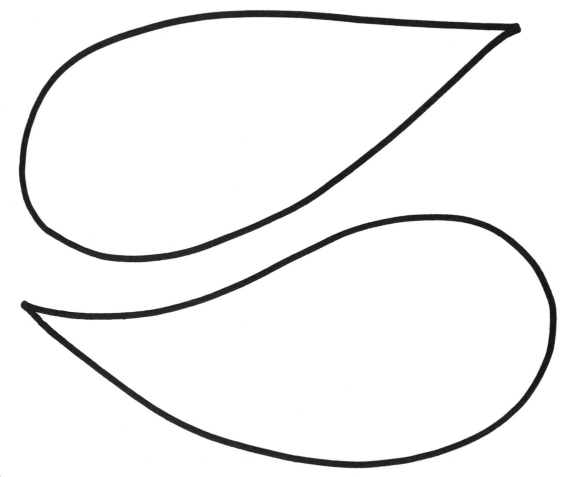

ME: _____ WHEN: _____

YOU: _____ WHERE: _____

US: _____

if we were stranded on a deserted island...

OUR ESSENTIALS

1.

2.

3.

ME: _____ WHEN: _____

You: _____ WHERE: _____

US: _____

our most
Frequently Asked Questions

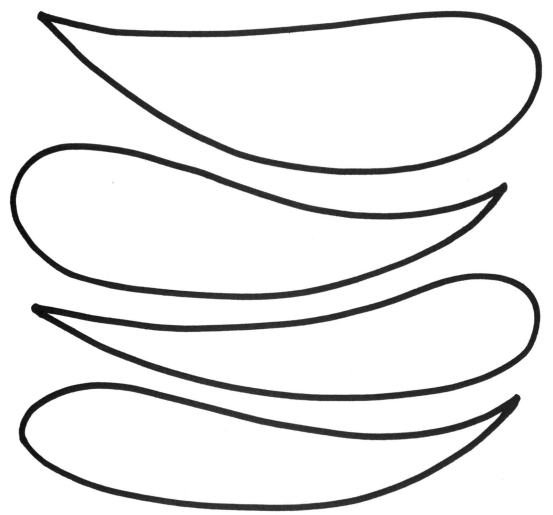

ME: _____ WHEN: _____

YOU: _____ WHERE: _____

US: _____

last time we got creative together

our masterpiece

ME: _____   WHEN: _____

YOU: _____   WHERE: _____

US: _____

challenges we helped each other through

1.

2.

3.

LEVEL COMPLETE!

ME: _____ WHEN: _____

You: _____ WHERE: _____

US: _____

how we celebrate the weekend

things we like about each other

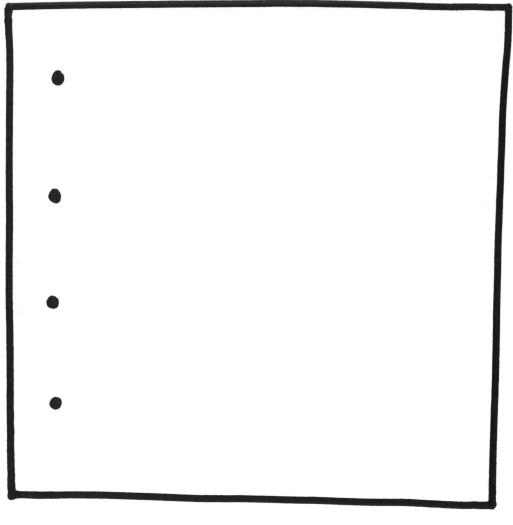

-
-
-
-

☐ in no particular order
☐ in a very particular order

ME: _____ WHEN: _____

You: _____ WHERE: _____

US: _____

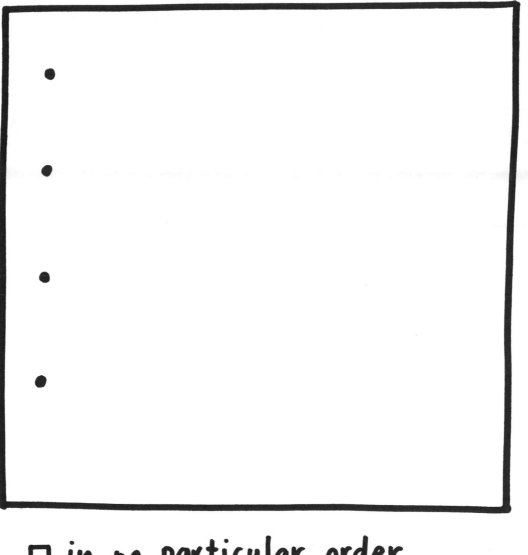

☐ in no particular order
☐ in a very particular order

ME: _____ WHEN: _____

YOU: _____ WHERE: _____

US: _____

our promises to
each other

- •
- •
- •
- •

SIGNED:

.... & ....

ME: _____ WHEN: _____

You: _____ WHERE: _____

US: _____

the things we share

MY STUFF

YOUR STUFF

ME: _____ WHEN: _____
You: _____ WHERE: _____
US: _____

we didn't want it to end!!

ME: _____ WHEN: _____

YOU: _____ WHERE: _____

US: _____

the members of our posse

ME: _____ WHEN: _____

YOU: _____ WHERE: _____

US: _____

three things we can both agree on

ME: _____ WHEN: _____

You: _____ WHERE: _____

US: _____

the perfect Halloween costumes for us

ME: _____ WHEN: _____

YOU: _____ WHERE: _____

US: _____

what we'll be doing
in 20 years

☐ safe prediction   ☐ wild guess

ME: _____   WHEN: _____

YOU: _____   WHERE: _____

US: _____

ideas for our matching tattoos

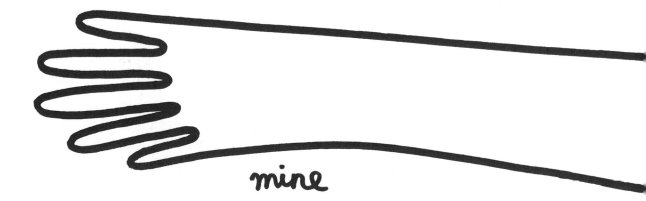

yours

mine

ME: _____ WHEN: _____
YOU: _____ WHERE: _____
US: _____

last time we had a two-person party

ME: _____ WHEN: _____

You: _____ WHERE: _____

US: _____

the homework we give each other

watch this:

read this:

search this:

ME: _____ WHEN: _____

You: _____ WHERE: _____

US: _____

things we both have on our bucket list

ME: _____ WHEN: _____

You: _____ WHERE: _____

US: _____

if we shared an online profile

 @

OUR BIO:

ME: _____   WHEN: _____

You: _____   WHERE: _____

US: _____

our best time in the sunshine

our best time in the rain

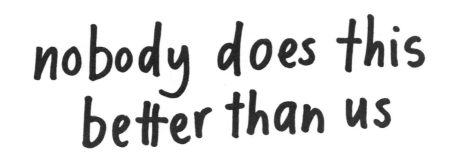

nobody does this better than us

ME: _____ WHEN: _____

You: _____ WHERE: _____

US: _____

our magic power

☐ cool ☐ wow ☐ dude! ☐ what?!?

ME: _____   WHEN: _____

YOU: _____   WHERE: _____

US: _____

how we exercise together

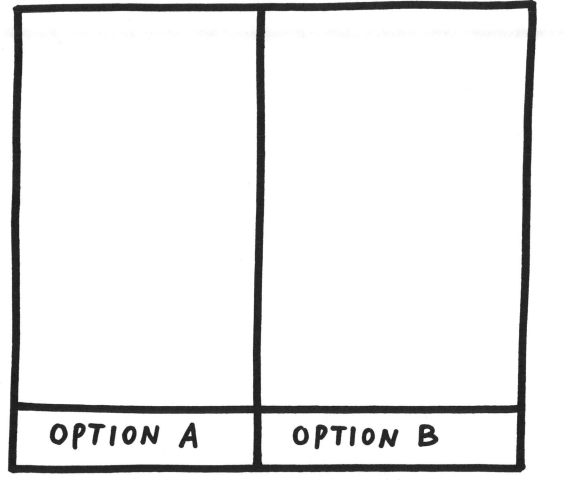

OPTION A	OPTION B

ME: _____   WHEN: _____

You: _____   WHERE: _____

US: _____

instructions for being as cool as we are

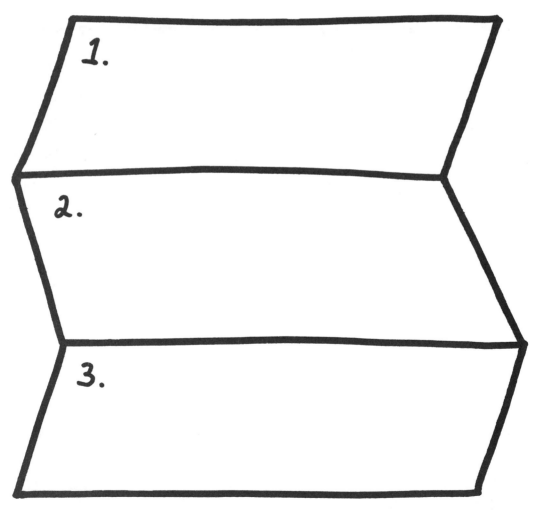

1.

2.

3.

ME: _____ WHEN: _____
YOU: _____ WHERE: _____
US: _____

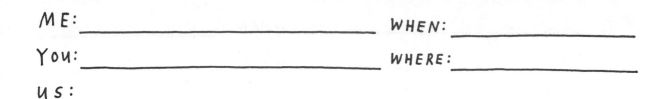

the last time we got a bit competitive

1ST

2ND

ME: _____   WHEN: _____

YOU: _____   WHERE: _____

US: _____

things we couldn't wait to tell each other

GOOD NEWS

1.

2.

3.

ME: _____   WHEN: _____

YOU: _____   WHERE: _____

US: _____

OUR YEARBOOK

YOU

most likely to:

....

....

most likely to:

ME

....

....

ME: _____ WHEN: _____

You: _____ WHERE: _____

US: _____

our greatest ever midnight snack

ME: _____   WHEN: _____

YOU: _____   WHERE: _____

US: _____

the chapters we've had together — so far!

I.

II.

III.

IV.

the best gifts we ever gave each other

TO:

FROM:

ME: _____ WHEN: _____

You: _____ WHERE: _____

US: _____

TO:
FROM:

ME: _____   WHEN: _____

You: _____   WHERE: _____

US: _____

our PERFECT day together

itinerery

8 AM:

3 PM:

10 PM:

ME: _____ WHEN: _____

YOU: _____ WHERE: _____

US: _____

the catchphrase we're famous for saying

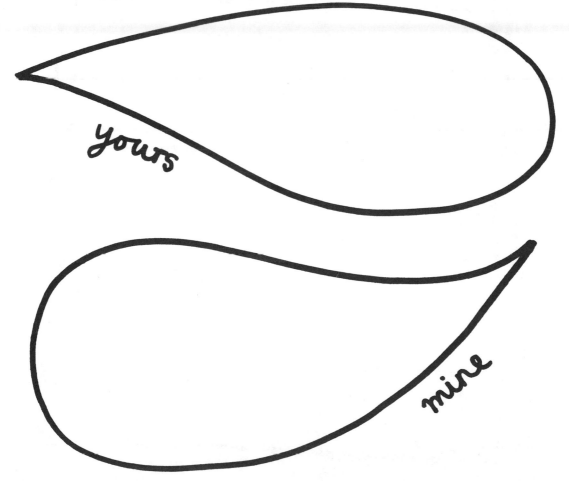

yours

mine

ME: _____ WHEN: _____

You: _____ WHERE: _____

US: _____

a moment we WISH
we got a photo of

X X

ME: _____   WHEN: _____

You: _____   WHERE: _____

US: _____

how to celebrate our next friendiversary

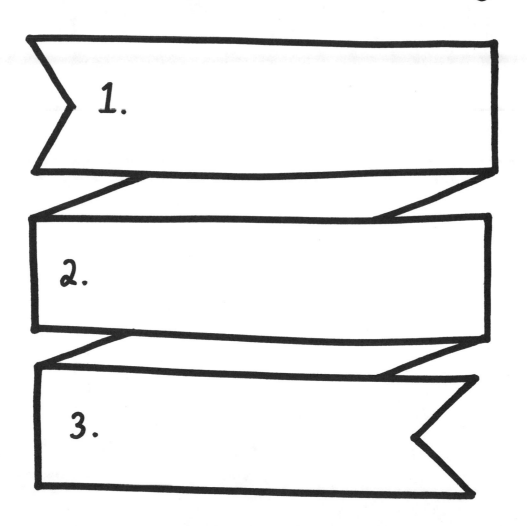

1.

2.

3.

the fan mail we'd write to each other

ME: _____   WHEN: _____

YOU: _____   WHERE: _____

US: _____

♡ HELLO!!!   ♡   ♡ ♡   ×× ☺

L♡VE always ×× YOUR BIGGEST FAN ××× ♡

ME: _____   WHEN: _____

You: _____   WHERE: _____

US: _____

okay, we'll just agree to disagree

ME: _____   WHEN: _____

You: _____   WHERE: _____

US: _____

the challenge we bravely accepted

I DARE YOU...

☐ PASS   ☐ FAIL   ☐ NICE TRY

ME: _____ WHEN: _____

You: _____ WHERE: _____

US: _____

the view from our favorite spot

ME: _____ WHEN: _____

You: _____ WHERE: _____

US: _____

new nicknames for each other

yours   mine

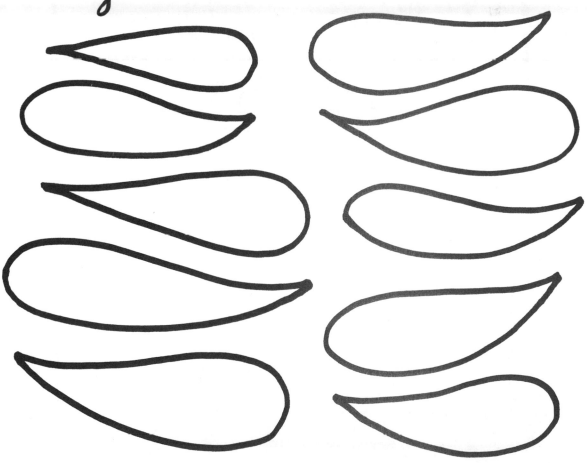

ME: _____ WHEN: _____

You: _____ WHERE: _____

US: _____

official police report

OUR CRIME
being too awesome

EVIDENCE

1.

2.

3.

ME: _____ WHEN: _____
You: _____ WHERE: _____
US: _____

my fortune for you

your fortune for me

ME: _____ WHEN: _____

You: _____ WHERE: _____

US: _____

our worst habits when we're together

1.

2.

3.

4.

* sorry, everyone!

ME: _____ WHEN: _____

YOU: _____ WHERE: _____

US: _____

the sure fire way
to cheer us up

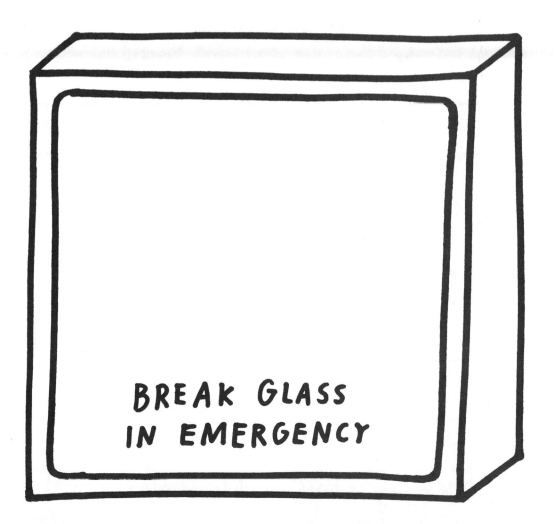

**BREAK GLASS
IN EMERGENCY**

ME: _____ WHEN: _____

YOU: _____ WHERE: _____

US: _____

our good deed
for the day

☐ loud & heroic   ☐ small & sweet

ME: _____   WHEN: _____

You: _____   WHERE: _____

US: _____

if we had our own reality TV show

EPISODE #1
HIGHLIGHTS

-
-
-
-

ME: _____ WHEN: _____

YOU: _____ WHERE: _____

US: _____

if Hollywood made a movie about us

TITLE:

STARRING:

as you

as me

ME: _____   WHEN: _____

YOU: _____   WHERE: _____

US: _____

things we think are
HILARIOUS*

1.

2.

3.

* even if no one else does.

our handmade cards
for each other

☐ special occasion   ☐ just because

ME: _____   WHEN: _____

YOU: _____   WHERE: _____

US: _____

☐ special occasion   ☐ just because

ME: _____ WHEN: _____

You: _____ WHERE: _____

US: _____

the crazy adventures we've had together

DANGER ZONE!

1.

2.

3.

ME: _____ WHEN: _____

YOU: _____ WHERE: _____

US: _____

our perfect movie night

+

snack selection:

ME: _____   WHEN: _____

You: _____   WHERE: _____

US: _____

what we protest about

NO MORE

WE WANT

ME: _____ WHEN: _____

You: _____ WHERE: _____

US: _____

our favorite kind of party

you're invited

WHAT:

WHERE:

PLEASE BRING:

ME: _____   WHEN: _____

You: _____   WHERE: _____

US: _____

a portrait of us

CHOOSE A THEME: ☐ fake beards
☐ the royal family   ☐ pirates!
☐ other _____

ME: _____ WHEN: _____

YOU: _____ WHERE: _____

US: _____

the mysteries we're trying to solve

HOW...

?

WHY...

?

WHO...

?

ME: _____ WHEN: _____

YOU: _____ WHERE: _____

US: _____

the most fun we could have in an hour

15 MINUTES

15 MINUTES

15 MINUTES

15 MINUTES

ME: _____ WHEN: _____

You: _____ WHERE: _____

US: _____

if our names were in the dictionary

_____

DEFINITION:

_____

DEFINITION:

ME: _____   WHEN: _____

You: _____   WHERE: _____

US: _____

little signs that we're growing up

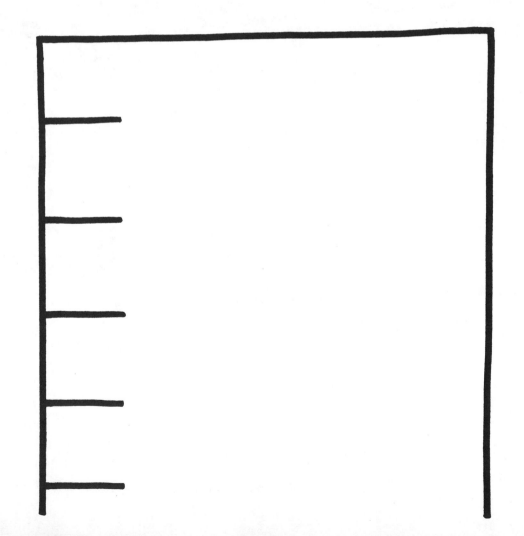

ME: _____   WHEN: _____

You: _____   WHERE: _____

US: _____

our recent words of wisdom

ME: _____   WHEN: _____

YOU: _____   WHERE: _____

US: _____

if we spend too much time together

SIDE EFFECTS

1.

2.

3.

ME: _____   WHEN: _____

You: _____   WHERE: _____

US: _____

our #1 move on the dancefloor

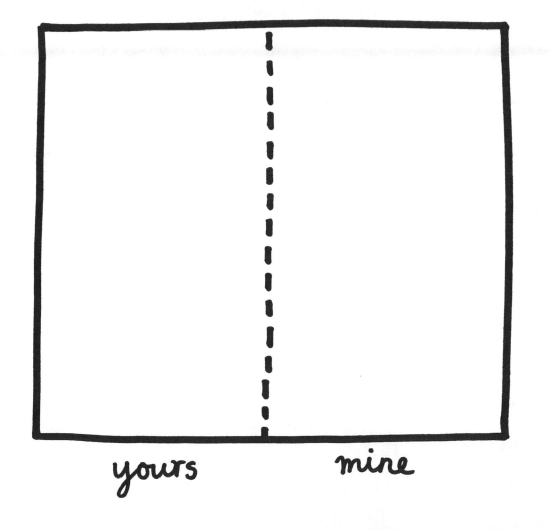

yours   mine

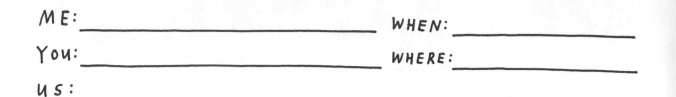

ME: _____ WHEN: _____

You: _____ WHERE: _____

US: _____

close-up details of us

ME: _____ WHEN: _____

You: _____ WHERE: _____

us: _____

how we celebrate the little things

our status updates

JUST NOW

ONE HOUR AGO

TWO HOURS AGO

YESTERDAY

ME: _____   WHEN: _____

YOU: _____   WHERE: _____

US: _____

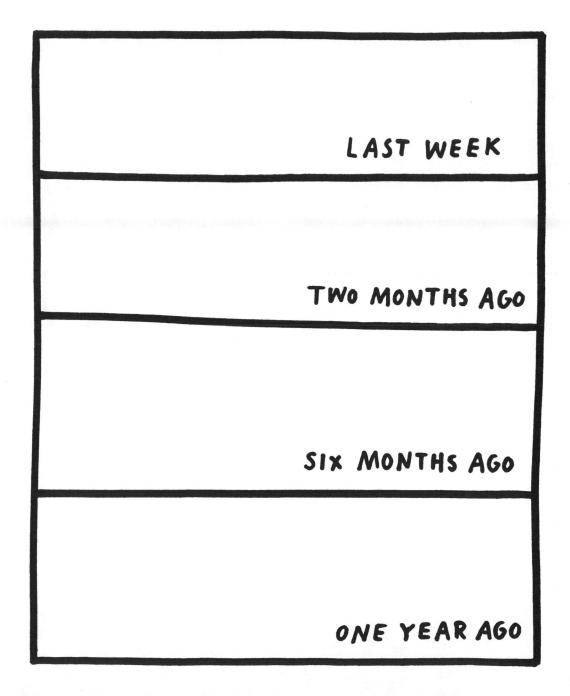

LAST WEEK

TWO MONTHS AGO

SIX MONTHS AGO

ONE YEAR AGO

ME: _____   WHEN: _____

YoU: _____   WHERE: _____

US: _____

times We've HAD FUN

times we've LOOKED COOL

ME: _____   WHEN: _____

YOU: _____   WHERE: _____

US: _____

how we cope when we're not together

1.

2.

3.

Wish you were Here xx

ME: _____   WHEN: _____

YOU: _____   WHERE: _____

US: _____

our recent teamwork

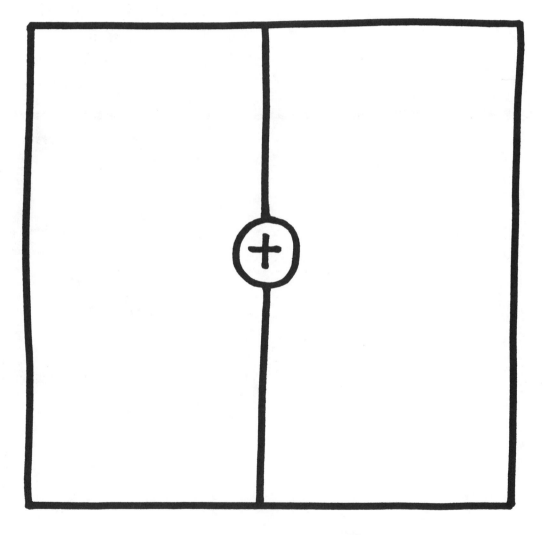

= WE DID IT!!

ME: _____   WHEN: _____
You: _____   WHERE: _____
US: _____

the internet stuff we send each other

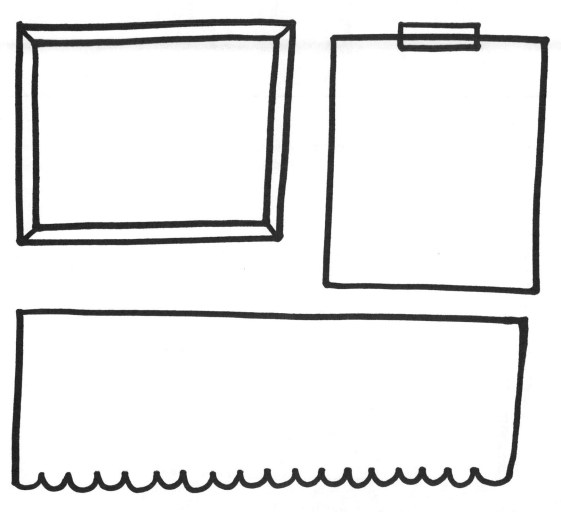

ME: _____   WHEN: _____

You: _____   WHERE: _____

US: _____

the last time we were treated extra-nice

VIP

ADMIT TWO

ME: _____   WHEN: _____

You: _____   WHERE: _____

US: _____

our own special recipe

☐ looks good   ☐ tastes good

☐ it's edible   ☐ no comment

the little ways we impress each other

YOUR REPORT CARD

A+

A+

A+

ME: _____   WHEN: _____
You: _____   WHERE: _____
US: _____

MY REPORT CARD

A+

A+

A+

ME: _____   WHEN: _____

You: _____   WHERE: _____

US: _____

our juicy secret

*** written in code words that
only we understand**

ME: _____ WHEN: _____

You: _____ WHERE: _____

US: _____

what our perfume would smell like

ME: _____ WHEN: _____

You: _____ WHERE: _____

US: _____

an incredibly good idea we had recently

TM ©

ME: _____   WHEN: _____

You: _____   WHERE: _____

US: _____

famous people we want in our clique

DEFINITELY	MAYBE

ME: _____ WHEN: _____

You: _____ WHERE: _____

US: _____

two truths and
one lie about us*

* in no particular order

ME: _____   WHEN: _____

You: _____   WHERE: _____

US: _____

detailed map of a walk we had together

ME: _____   WHEN: _____

You: _____   WHERE: _____

US: _____

our new tradition

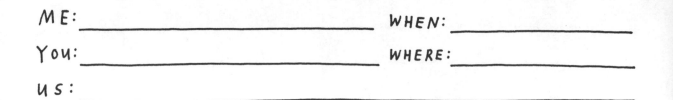

every... ☐ morning ☐ afternoon
☐ Tuesday ☐ full moon ☐_____

ME: _____ WHEN: _____

You: _____ WHERE: _____

US: _____

the story we'll tell when we're old and gray

remember
that time we...

ME: _____   WHEN: _____

You: _____   WHERE: _____

US: _____

the last reason we did these things

HUG	
HIGH FIVE	
SCREAM	
HAPPY DANCE	

ME: _____ WHEN: _____

You: _____ WHERE: _____

US: _____

the gibberish we speak

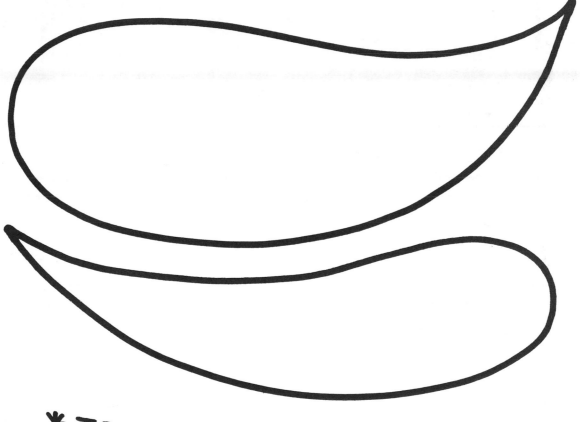

* TRANSLATION:

our mixtapes for
each other

listen to this when:

ME: _____   WHEN: _____

YOU: _____   WHERE: _____

US: _____

listen to this when:

ME: _____ WHEN: _____

You: _____ WHERE: _____

US: _____

things we never get bored of

1.

2.

3.

ME: _____ WHEN: _____

You: _____ WHERE: _____

US: _____

the book we could write together

☐ SELF-HELP   ☐ DIY   ☐ COOKBOOK

☐ OTHER _____

ME: _____ WHEN: _____

YOU: _____ WHERE: _____

US: _____

that thing we said we'd do one day

ME: _____ WHEN: _____

You: _____ WHERE: _____

US: _____

our favorite game to play

THE RULES

-
-
-

ME: _____   WHEN: _____

You: _____   WHERE: _____

US: _____

deciding our next move

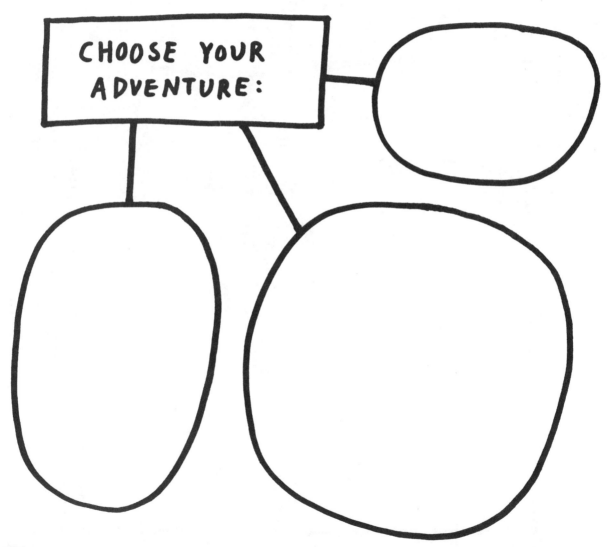

CHOOSE YOUR
ADVENTURE:

ME: _____ WHEN: _____

You: _____ WHERE: _____

US: _____

these are a few of our favorite things

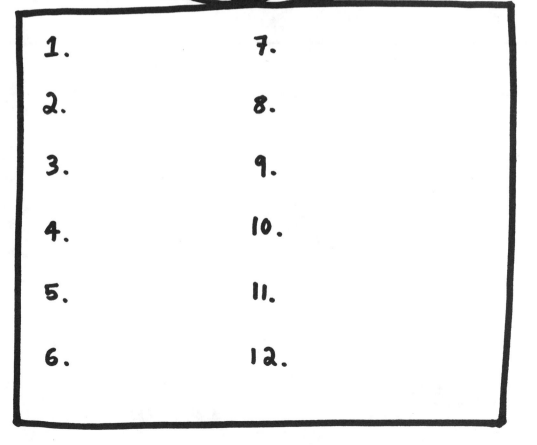

1.

2.

3.

4.

5.

6.

7.

8.

9.

10.

11.

12.

ME: _____   WHEN: _____

You: _____   WHERE: _____

US: _____

our recent transformation

BEFORE

AFTER

ME: _____   WHEN: _____

YOU: _____   WHERE: _____

US: _____

the yummiest meals we've had together

ME: _____ WHEN: _____

You: _____ WHERE: _____

US: _____

the last time we had fun trying

PARTICIPATION AWARD

ME: _____ WHEN: _____

YOU: _____ WHERE: _____

US: _____

our favorite things
to chat about

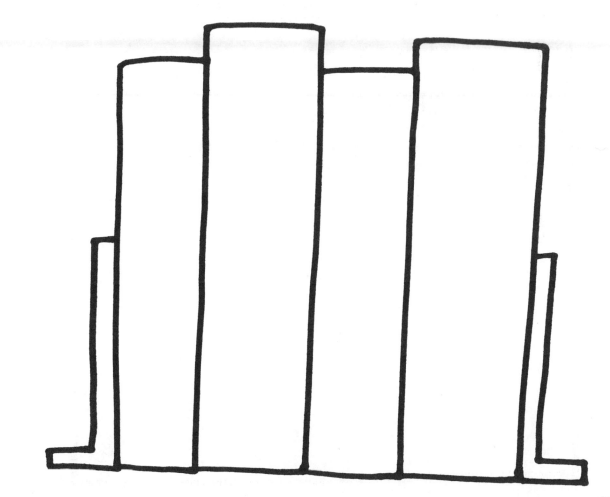

ME: _____   WHEN: _____

YOU: _____   WHERE: _____

US: _____

the secret business
we do together

Please
DO NOT DISTURB

ME: _____   WHEN: _____

You: _____   WHERE: _____

US: _____

our current obsession

xx

ME: _____   WHEN: _____
You: _____   WHERE: _____
US: _____

how we get ready to go out

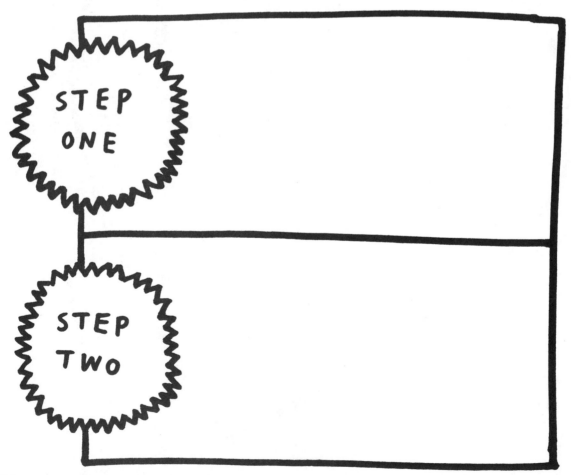

STEP ONE

STEP TWO

ME: _____ WHEN: _____

You: _____ WHERE: _____

US: _____

the name of our
secret club

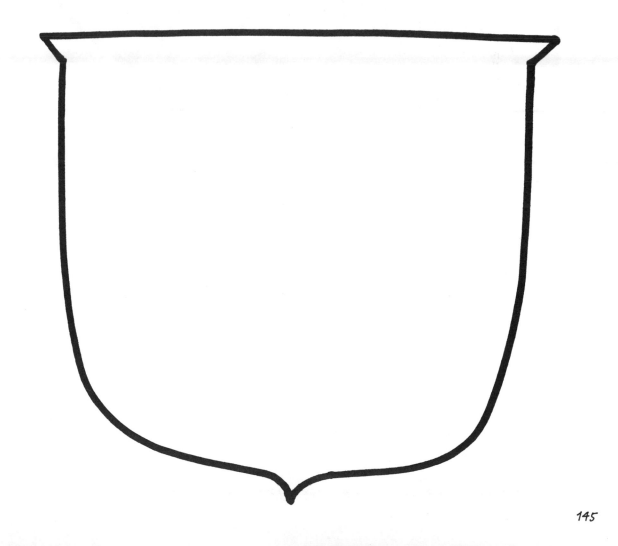

our ongoing debate

ME: _____ WHEN: _____

YOU: _____ WHERE: _____

US: _____

how we make our own fun

supplies:

directions:

1.

2.

3.

ME: _____ WHEN: _____

You: _____ WHERE: _____

US: _____

our recent questions
about life and love

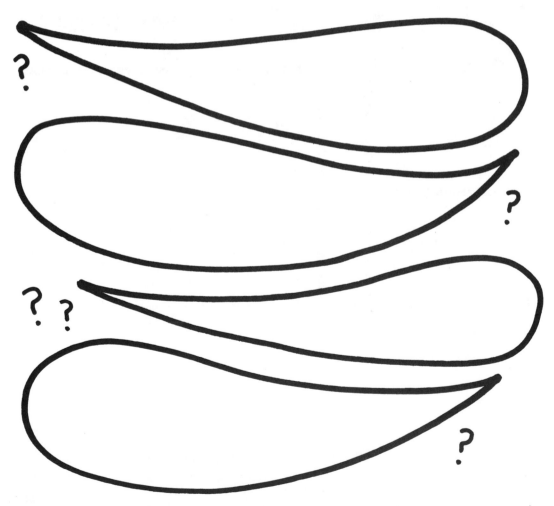

ME: _____ WHEN: _____

You: _____ WHERE: _____

US: _____

something we're REALLY looking forward to

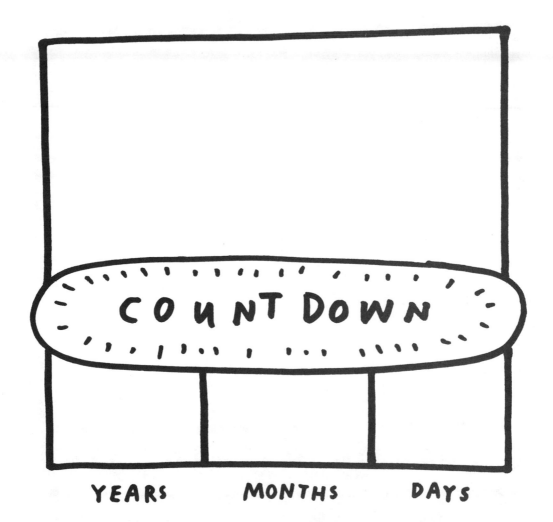

COUNTDOWN

YEARS   MONTHS   DAYS

ME: _____ WHEN: _____

You: _____ WHERE: _____

US: _____

the life lesson we learned together

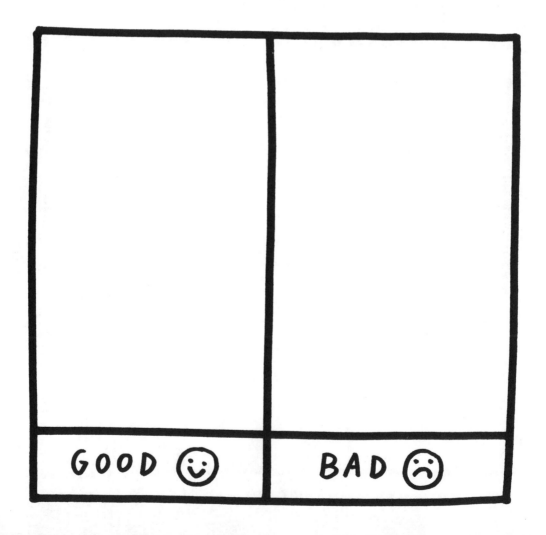

GOOD 😊   BAD 🙁

ME: _____ WHEN: _____

YOU: _____ WHERE: _____

US: _____

the last time we got FREE STUFF

ME: _____   WHEN: _____

You: _____   WHERE: _____

US: _____

the recipe for us

ingredients

directions

1.

2.

3.

ME: _____ WHEN: _____

YOU: _____ WHERE: _____

US: _____

our motto for life

ME: _____   WHEN: _____

You: _____   WHERE: _____

US: _____

unspoken rules we both seem to agree on

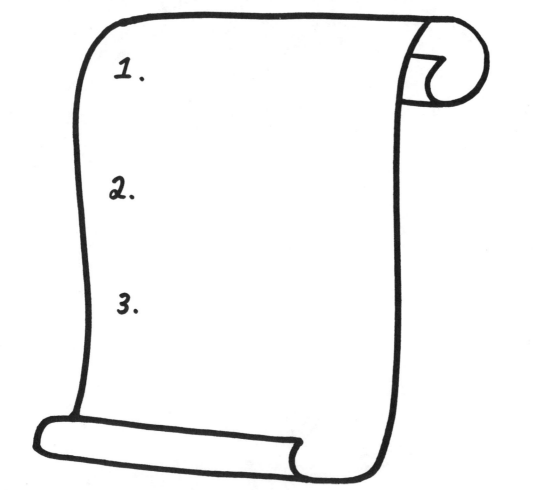

1.

2.

3.

ME: _____ WHEN: _____

You: _____ WHERE: _____

US: _____

our superpowers

YOURS   MINE

ME: _____   WHEN: _____

You: _____   WHERE: _____

US: _____

our earliest memories of each other

ARCHIVE

1.

2.

3.

ME: _____ WHEN: _____

You: _____ WHERE: _____

US: _____

if we made our own
ice cream flavor

ME: _____   WHEN: _____

You: _____   WHERE: _____

US: _____

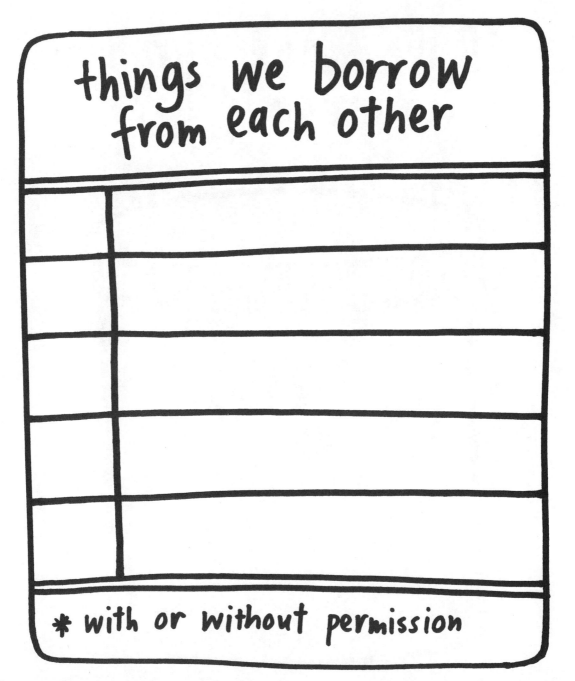

things we borrow
from each other

* with or without permission

ME: _____   WHEN: _____

You: _____   WHERE: _____

US: _____

our proof that opposites attract

you

me

ME: _____   WHEN: _____

YOU: _____   WHERE: _____

US: _____

the BIGGEST event
we've been to

ADMIT TWO

and the
smallest
event

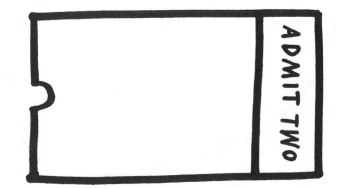

ADMIT TWO

ME: _____   WHEN: _____

You: _____   WHERE: _____

US: _____

something we changed our minds about

BEFORE   AFTER

ME: _____ WHEN: _____

You: _____ WHERE: _____

US: _____

little souvenirs we've collected together

1.

2.

3.

ME: _____   WHEN: _____

YOU: _____   WHERE: _____

US: _____

our favorite way to procrastinate

TO DO

ME: _____   WHEN: _____

You: _____   WHERE: _____

US: _____

things we'd like to steal from each other

ME: _____   WHEN: _____

YOU: _____   WHERE: _____

US: _____

that little thing we made a BIG deal about

CONGRATULATIONS!!

what our best wrestling move would be

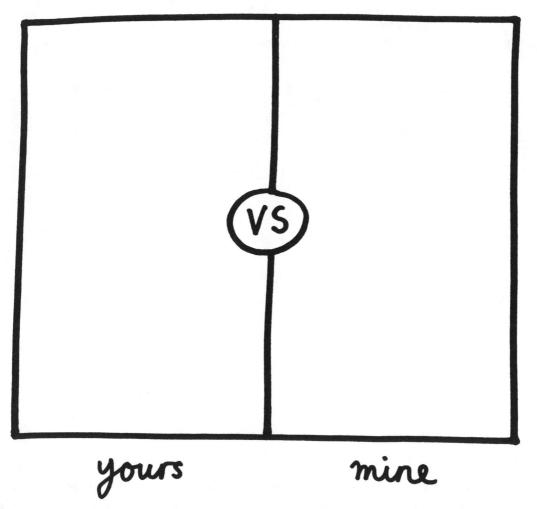

yours   mine

ME: _____ WHEN: _____

YOU: _____ WHERE: _____

US: _____

the moment we felt closest to each other

*aww!

ME: _____   WHEN: _____

You: _____   WHERE: _____

US: _____

our most casual
time together

our most fancy time together

ME: _____   WHEN: _____

YOU: _____   WHERE: _____

US: _____

our first impressions of each other

ME: _____   WHEN: _____

You: _____   WHERE: _____

US: _____

new things we've tried recently

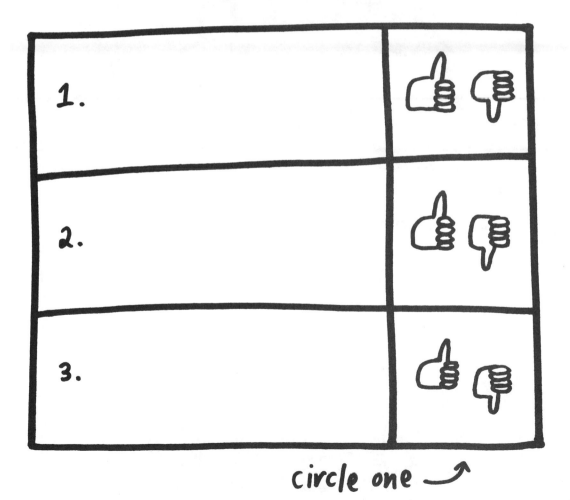

1.	👍 👎
2.	👍 👎
3.	👍 👎

circle one ↗

ME: _____   WHEN: _____

You: _____   WHERE: _____

US: _____

our ^unofficial world records

1.

2.

3.

ME: _____ WHEN: _____

You: _____ WHERE: _____

US: _____

little ways we make each other smile

ME: _____ WHEN: _____

You: _____ WHERE: _____

US: _____

ways we've become
the same

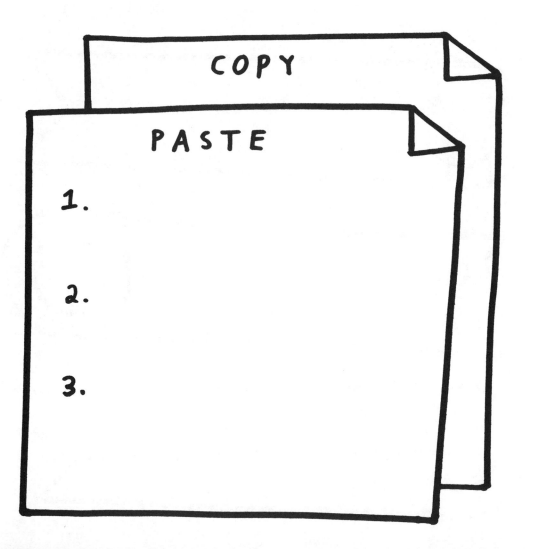

COPY

PASTE

1.

2.

3.

ME: _____   WHEN: _____

You: _____   WHERE: _____

US: _____

our happy place

OPENING
HOURS:

ME: _____   WHEN: _____

YOU: _____   WHERE: _____

US: _____

if this was our restaurant...

menu

entrée:

dinner:

dessert:

drink:

ME: _____ WHEN: _____

You: _____ WHERE: _____

US: _____

messages from our inbox

highlights of our time together -so far!

THEN

ME: _____ WHEN: _____

You: _____ WHERE: _____

US: _____

NOW

ME: _____   WHEN: _____

YOU: _____   WHERE: _____

US: _____

a small "thanks" we forgot to tell each other

thank you!   xx

thank you!   xx

ME: _____   WHEN: _____

You: _____   WHERE: _____

US: _____

last time we didn't act our age

☐ like little kids   ☐ like old people

what our fairytale ending would look like

ME: _____ WHEN: _____

YOU: _____ WHERE: _____

US: _____

... and we all lived happily
ever after. The End.

ABOUT THE AUTHOR

Lisa Currie is the author of The Scribble Diary.
Her hometown is Melbourne, Australia, but she's probably
not there right now.

Visit her online: lisacurrie.com

thank you!!

A big thank you to the team at Perigee
Books. Especially to my editor, Meg Leder.
Thanks also to my agent, Sorche Fairbank.

Much love to my family and friends!
Especially to my mum, Sue Currie, for your
unwaivering support and kindness. ♡
Thank you to Leonie Bourke for welcoming
me into your home while I created this book.

To every scribbler who's joined me on the
Scribble Project blog over the years: your
beautiful handiwork and wild minds will
forever delight me! Thank you for that.

OTHER BOOKS by LISA CURRIE

Available at all good bookstores!

the positivity kit

A creative space for you to draw, write, doodle over, and cut and paste. Soon it'll be a handmade map that can guide you back to your happiest self, back to your sweet spot in life, whenever you need it.

SURPRISE yourself

Turn every day into a new beginning with this DIY happiness guide that will get you out of your head and into the world. Ready to try something new? Flip to any page and begin . . .

the scribble diary

Welcome to your own playful, personal doodling space—to vent your thoughts, reflect on your day, and jot down what's in your brain right now.